The T♡ddler's handb◉◉k

with over **100 Words** that every kid should know

BY DAYNA MARTIN

INGLES/FILIPINO

ENGAGE BOOKS
VANCOUVER

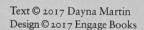
ENGAGE BOOKS

Mailing address
PO BOX 4608
Main Station Terminal
349 West Georgia Street
Vancouver, BC
Canada, V6B 4A1

www.engagebooks.ca

Written & compiled by: Dayna Martin
Edited & translated by: A.R. Roumanis
Proofread by: Dorina Tuazon
Designed by: A.R. Roumanis
Photos supplied by: Shutterstock
Photo on page 47 by: Faye Cornish

FIRST EDITION / FIRST PRINTING

LIBRARY AND ARCHIVES CANADA CATALOGUING IN PUBLICATION

Martin, Dayna, 1983–, author
    The toddler's handbook : numbers, colors, shapes, sizes, ABC animals, opposites, and sounds, with over 100 words that every kid should know / written by Dayna Martin ; edited by A.R. Roumanis.

Issued in print and electronic formats.
Text in English and Filipino.
ISBN 978-1-77226-433-3 (bound). –
ISBN 978-1-77226-434-0 (paperback). –
ISBN 978-1-77226-435-7 (pdf). –
ISBN 978-1-77226-436-4 (epub). –
ISBN 978-1-77226-437-1 (kindle)

1. Filipino language – Vocabulary – Juvenile literature.
2. Vocabulary – Juvenile literature.
3. Word recognition – Juvenile literature.
I. Martin, Dayna, 1983– . Toddler's handbook.
II. Martin, Dayna, 1983– . Toddler's handbook. Filipino.
III. Title.

PL5665.25.M37 2017   J499'.21181   C2017-905756-11
                                              C2017-905757-X

Aa
Alligator

Buwaya

Bb
Bear

Oso

Cc
Cat

Pusa

4

Dog

Dd

Aso

Fox

Ff

Soro

Elephant

Ee

Elepante

Goat

Gg

Kambing 5

Horse

Hh

Kabayo

Iguana

Ii

Iguana

Jj

Jaguar

Jaguar

6

Koala

Kk

Koala

Lion

Ll

Leon

Mouse

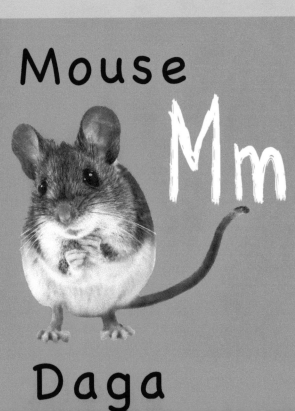

Mm

Daga

Newt

Nn

Newt

7

Otter

Oo

Oter

Pig

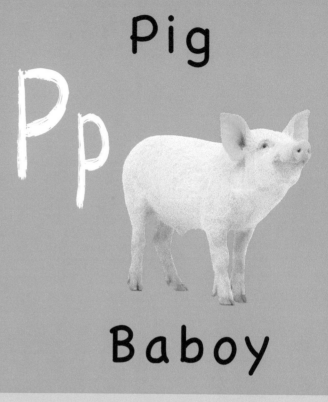

Pp

Baboy

Quail

Qq

8   Pugo

Rabbit

Rr

Kuneho

Seal

S s

Seal

Tiger

T t

Tigre

Uakari

U u

Uakari

Vulture

V v

Buwitre 9

Weasel

Ww

Weasel

X-ray fish

Xx

Pristella maxillaris

Yak

Yy

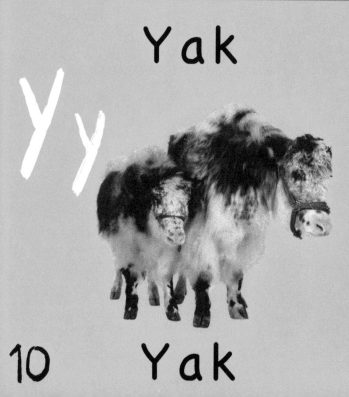

Yak

Zebra

Zz

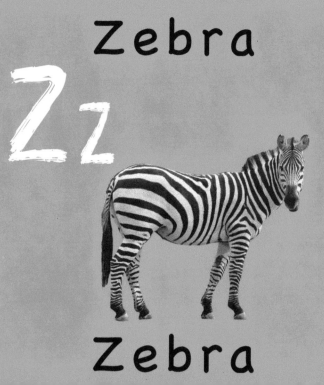

Zebra

Apple

One
1
Isa

Mansanas

Crackers

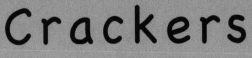

Two
2
Dalawa

Kraker

Watermelon slices

Three
3
Tatlo

Mga hiwa ng pakwan

11

Strawberries

Four
4
Apat

Strawberry

Carrots

Five
5
Lima

Karot

Tomatoes

Six
6
Anim

12

Kamatis

Squash

Seven

7

Pito

Kalabasa

Fruit slices

Eight

8

walo

Mga hiwa ng prutas

Potatoes

Nine

9

Siyam

Patatas

Cookies

Ten

10

Sampu

Kukis

13

Rainbow

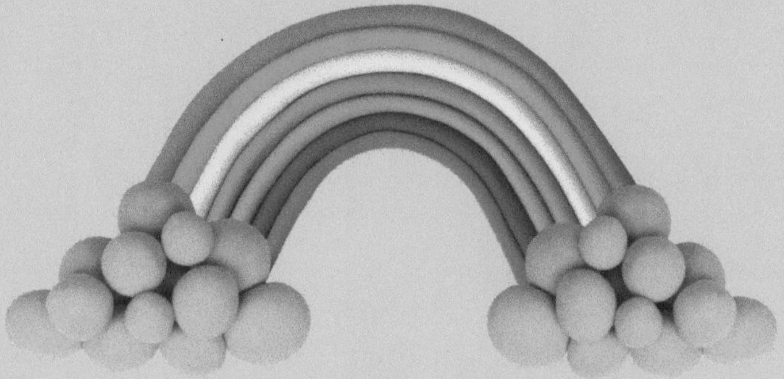

Bahaghari

Red

Pula

Orange

14 Orange

Yellow

Dilaw

Green
Berde

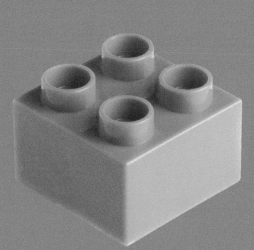

Blue
Asul

Indigo
Indigo

Violet
Lila

15

Up

Taas

Down
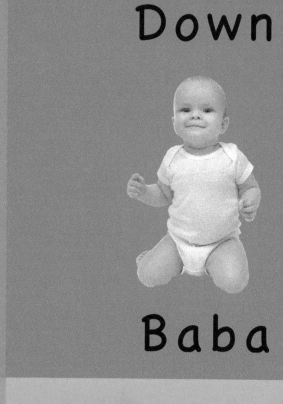
Baba

In

16 Sa loob

Out

Labas

Hot
Cold

Mainit
Malamig

Wet
Dry

Basa
Tuyo

Front

Harap

Back

Likod

On

Buksan

Off

Patayin

18

Open

Bukas

Closed

Sarado

Empty
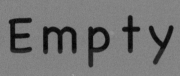

Walang laman

Full

Puno

19

Safe

Ligtas

Dangerous

Delikado

Big

Malaki

Small

Maliit

20

Asleep
Awake

Tulog

Gising

Long
Short

Mahaba

Maikli

21

Circle

Bilog

Square

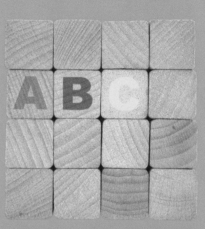

Parisukat

Triangle

22 Tatsulok

Rectangle

Parihaba

Diamond

Hugis-diyamante

Star

Hugis-bituin

Oval

Oval

Heart

Hugis-puso 23

Sneeze

Ah-choo

Hatsing

Bahin

Duck

Quack

Kwak

Pato

Cow

Moo

Maa

24 Baka

Phone

Ring

kring

Telepono

Monkey

Ooh-
ooh-
ahh-
ahh

hoo-
hoo-
aah-

Unggoy

Frog

Ribbit

Kokak

Palaka

Hush

Shh

Sshhh

Patahimikin 25

Rooster

cock-a-doodle-doo

Tiktilaok

Tandang

Drums

Boom

Boom

Tambol

Snake

Hiss

Sssssss

Ahas

Owl
Hoot
Hoot
Kuwago

Bumblebee
BUZZ
BZZZZZZ
Bubuyog

Hands
Clap
Palakpak
Kamay

Lamb
Baa
Ong
Tupa

27

Crawl
Gumapang

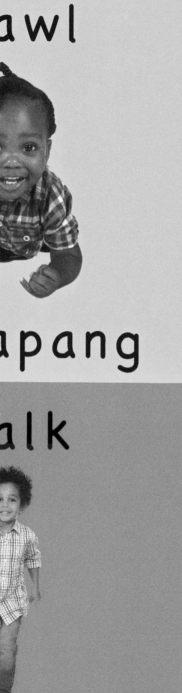

Roll
Gumulong

Walk
Lumakad

Run
Tumakbo

Hop

Lumukso

Ride

Sumakay

Kiss

Humalik

Jump

Tumalon

Happy
Masaya

Sad
Malungkot

Angry
Galit

Scared

Takot

Frustration

Pagkabigo

Surprise

Gulat

Shock

Shock

Brave

Matapang 31

Baseball

Baseball

Basketball

Basketball

Tennis

32 Tennis

Soccer

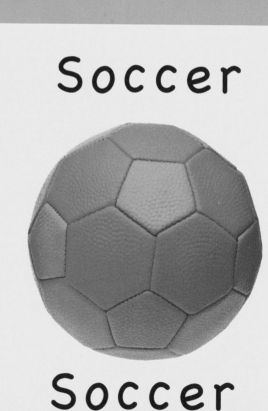

Soccer

Badminton

Football

Badminton

Football

Volleyball

Golf

Volleyball

Golf

33

Fire truck

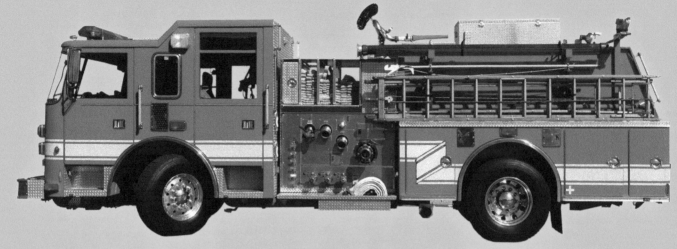

Trak ng bumbero

Car

Truck

34 Kotse

Trak

Helicopter

Helicopter

Airplane

Eroplano

Train

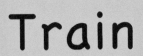

Tren

Boat

Bangka 35

Small   Medium   Large

Maliit Katamtaman Malaki

Small   Medium   Large

36 Maliit Katamtaman Malaki

Large Medium Small

Malaki Katamtaman Maliit

Large Medium Small

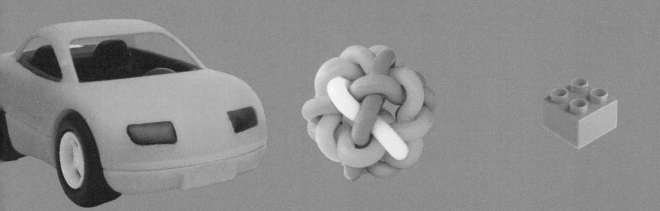

Malaki Katamtaman Maliit

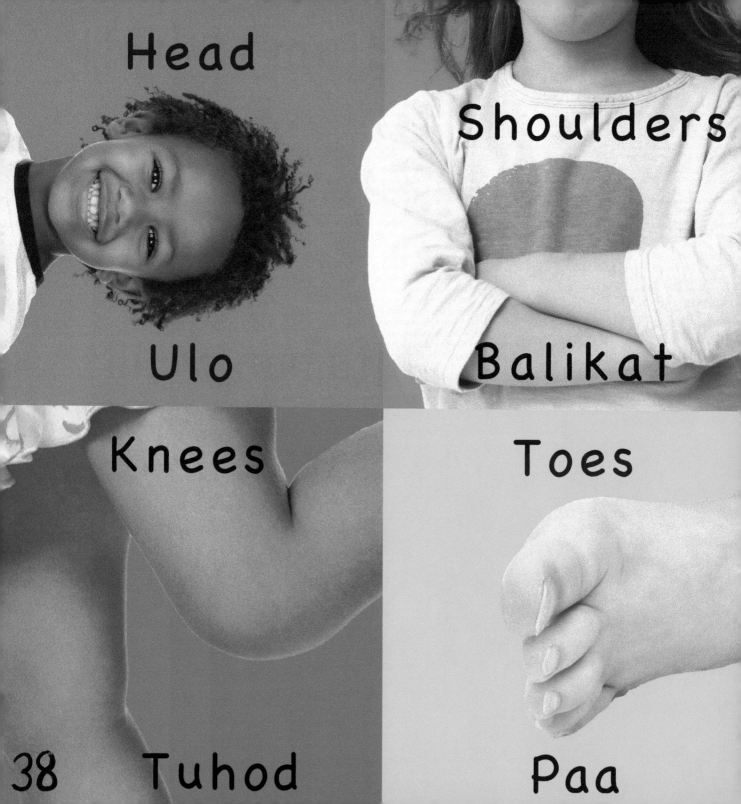

Head

Ulo

Shoulders

Balikat

Knees

Tuhod

Toes

Paa

38

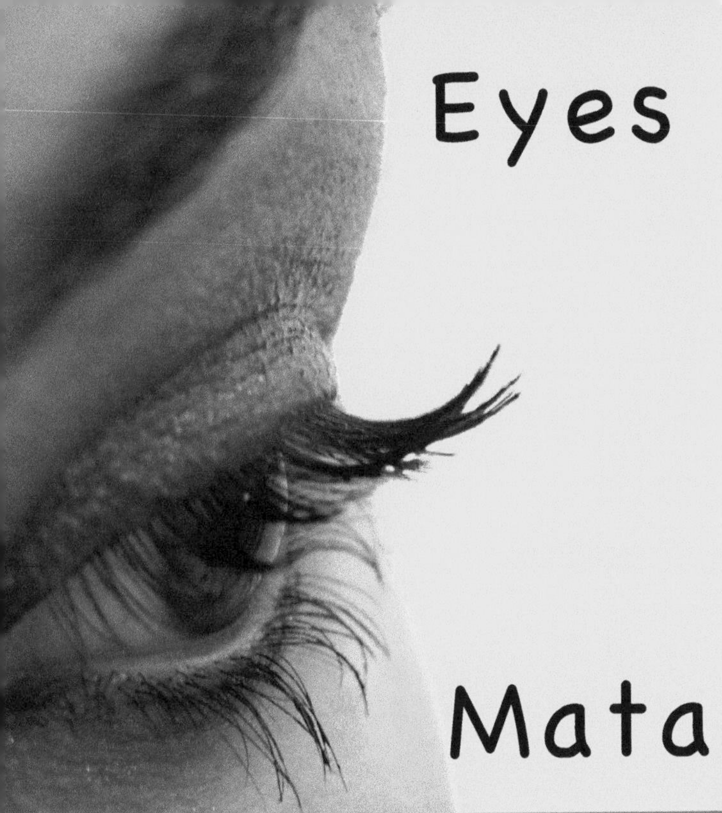

Eyes

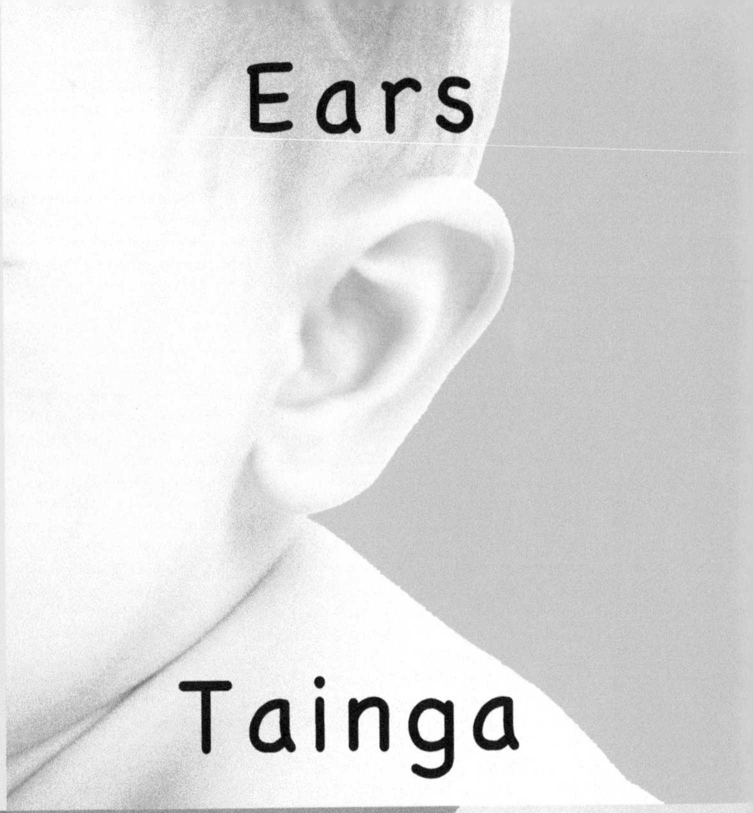

Ears

Mata

Tainga

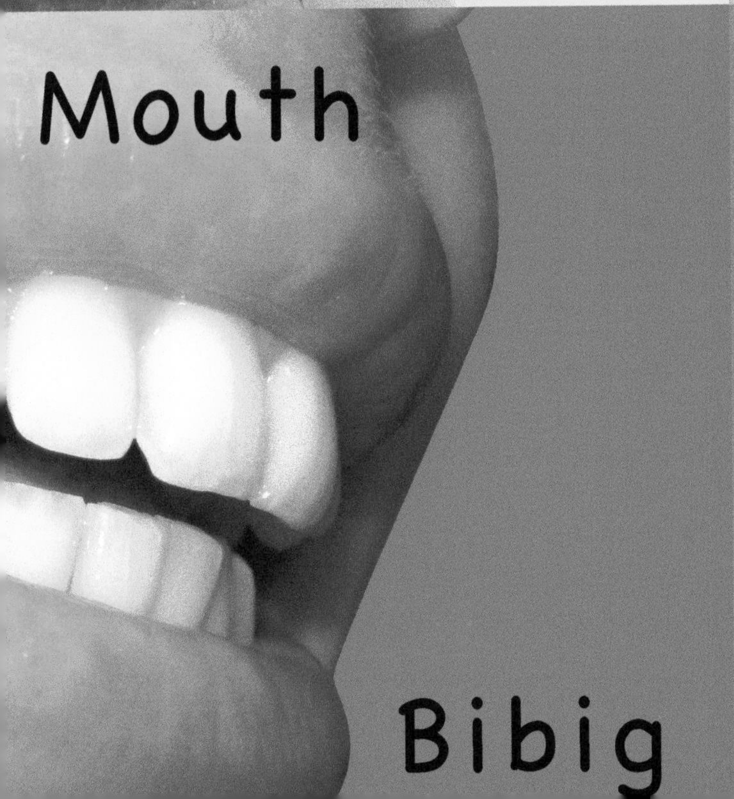

Mouth

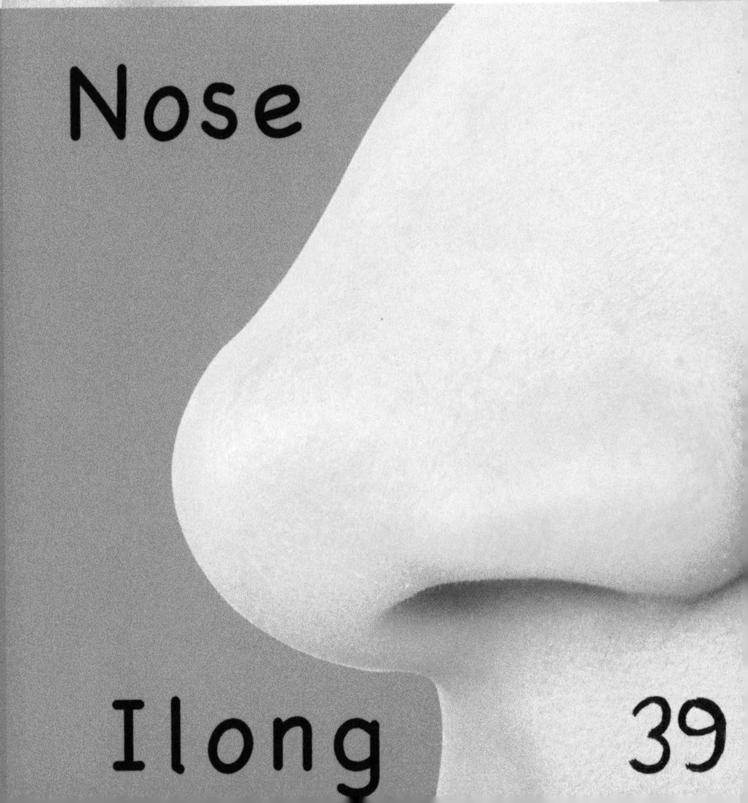

Nose

Bibig

Ilong

39

Sippy cup
Baso

Bowl
Mangkok

Pot
40 Palayok

Cup
Tasa

Plate
Plato

Fork
Tinidor

Knife
Kutsilyo

Spoon
Kutsara 41

Hat

Sombrero

Shirt

Kamiseta

Pants

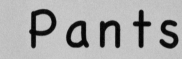

42 Pantalon

Shorts

Shorts

Gloves

Guwantes

Sunglasses

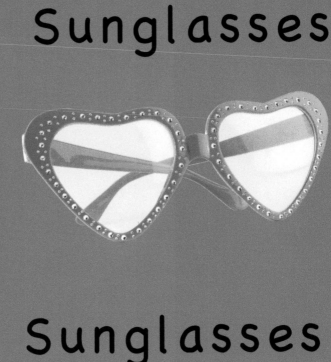

Sunglasses

Socks

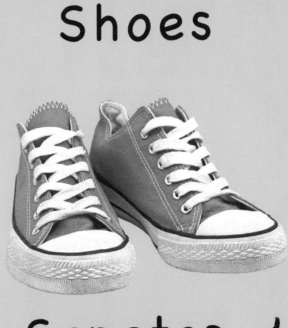

Medyas

Shoes

Sapatos   43

Bath time
Oras ng pagligo

Paliguan

Soap

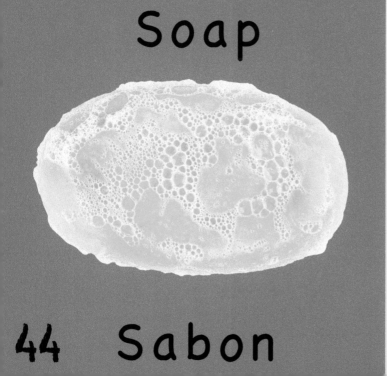

Sabon

Towel

Tuwalya

Brush

Magsipilyo

Book

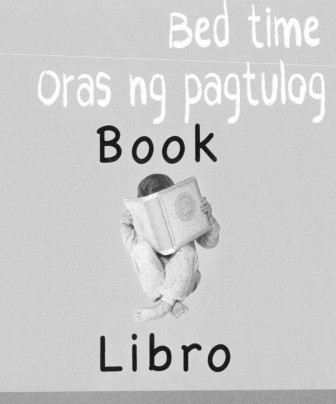

Libro

Potty

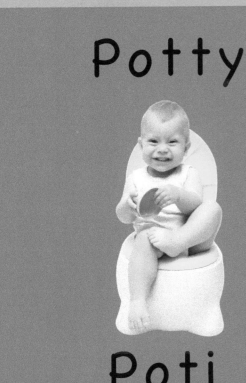

Poti

Bed

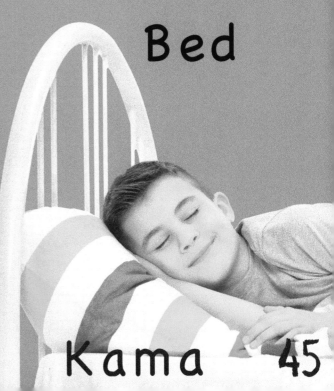

Kama

45

The Toddler's Handbook

activity / aktibidad

Match the following to the pictures below. Can you find **7 squash, a hooting owl, a rainbow, a baseball, a lion, square blocks, a sad boy, a helicopter, and shoes?**

Itugma ang mga sumusunod sa mga larawan sa ibaba. Maaari kang makahanap ng **7 kalabasa, isang kuwago, isang bahaghari, isang baseball, isang leon, mga blokeng parisukat, isang malungkot na bata, isang helicopter, at sapatos?**

helicopter / helicopter

shoes / sapatos

hooting owl / kuwago

baseball / baseball

7 squash / 7 kalabasa

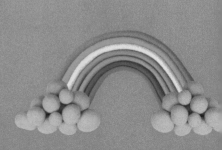

sad boy / isang malungkot na bata

lion / leon

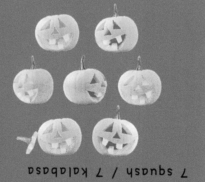

square blocks / mga blokeng parisukat

rainbow / bahaghari

46

Find more early concept books at www.engagebooks.ca

The Baby's handbook — With over 20 songs that every kid should know
DIDDLE · ITSY BITSY · TEA POT · TWINKLE · ...KEN DRUM · MUFFIN MAN · ...ACDONALD · MULBERRY · ...ROCK-A-BY · HICKORY · LITTLE LAMB · PAT-A-CAKE

The Preschooler's handbook — With over 300 Words that every kid should know
ABCs · NUMBERS · COLORS · SHAPES · MUSIC · SCHOOL · MANNERS · MATCHING · JOBS · ARTS · BRUSH TEETH · POTTY

The Kindergartener's handbook — With over 300 Words that every kid should know
ABCs · COLORS · MATH · SHAPES · VOWELS · TIME · SEASONS · SENSES · WEATHER · RHYMES · SCHOOL · CHORES

About the Author

Dayna Martin is the mother of three young boys. When she finished writing *The Toddler's Handbook* her oldest son was 18 months old, and she had newborn twins. Following the successful launch of her first book, Dayna began work on *The Baby's Handbook*, *The Preschooler's Handbook*, and *The Kindergartener's Handbook*. The ideas in her books were inspired by her search to find better ways to teach her children. The concepts were vetted by numerous educators in different grade levels. Dayna is a stay-at-home mom, and is passionate about teaching her children in innovative ways. Her experiences have inspired her to create resources to help other families. With thousands of copies sold, her books have already become a staple learning source for many children around the world.

Translations

ARABIC	JAPANESE
DUTCH	KOREAN
FILIPINO	MANDARIN
FRENCH	POLISH
GERMAN	PORTUGUESE
GREEK	RUSSIAN
HEBREW	SPANISH
HINDI	VIETNAMESE
ITALIAN	

Have comments or suggestions?
Contact us at: alexis@engagebooks.ca

 Show us how you enjoy your #handbook. Tweet a picture to @engagebooks for a chance to win free prizes.

47

CPSIA information can be obtained
at www.ICGtesting.com
Printed in the USA
LVHW071745050421
683466LV00012B/861